MY FIRST SPORTS

Hockey

by Ray McClellan

BLASTOFF! READERS 4

BELLWETHER MEDIA • MINNEAPOLIS, MN

Note to Librarians, Teachers, and Parents:

Blastoff! Readers are carefully developed by literacy experts and combine standards-based content with developmentally appropriate text.

Level 1 provides the most support through repetition of high-frequency words, light text, predictable sentence patterns, and strong visual support.

Level 2 offers early readers a bit more challenge through varied simple sentences, increased text load, and less repetition of high-frequency words.

Level 3 advances early-fluent readers toward fluency through increased text and concept load, less reliance on visuals, longer sentences, and more literary language.

Level 4 builds reading stamina by providing more text per page, increased use of punctuation, greater variation in sentence patterns, and increasingly challenging vocabulary.

Level 5 encourages children to move from "learning to read" to "reading to learn" by providing even more text, varied writing styles, and less familiar topics.

Whichever book is right for your reader, Blastoff! Readers are the perfect books to build confidence and encourage a love of reading that will last a lifetime!

This edition first published in 2010 by Bellwether Media, Inc.

No part of this publication may be reproduced in whole or in part without written permission of the publisher. For information regarding permission, write to Bellwether Media, Inc., Attention: Permissions Department, Post Office Box 19349, Minneapolis, MN 55419.

Library of Congress Cataloging-in-Publication Data
McClellan, Ray.
   Hockey / by Ray McClellan.
      p. cm. – (Blastoff! readers. My first sports)
   Includes bibliographical references and index.
   Summary: "Simple text and full color photographs introduce beginning readers to the sport of hockey. Developed by literacy experts for students in grades two through five"–Provided by publisher.
   ISBN 978-1-60014-330-4 (hardcover : alk. paper)
   1. Hockey–Juvenile literature. I. Title.

GV847.25.M335 2009
796.962–dc22

                              2009008180

Contents

What Is Hockey?

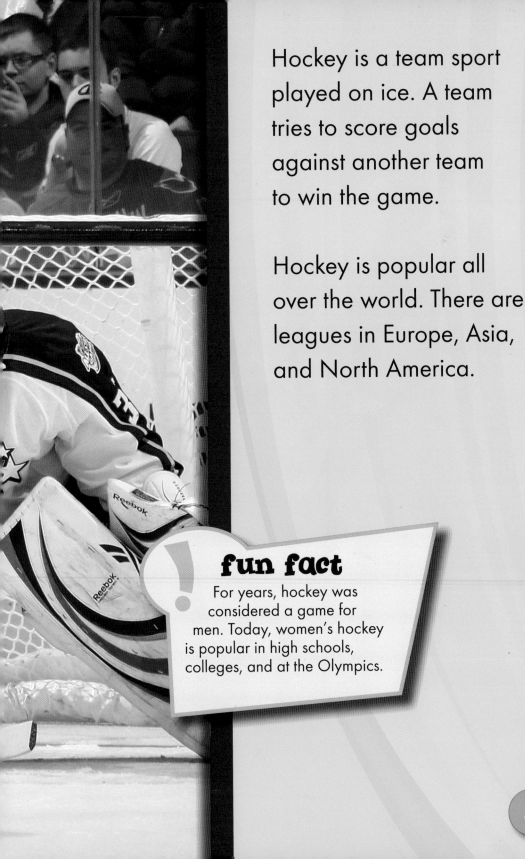

Hockey is a team sport played on ice. A team tries to score goals against another team to win the game.

Hockey is popular all over the world. There are leagues in Europe, Asia, and North America.

fun fact

For years, hockey was considered a game for men. Today, women's hockey is popular in high schools, colleges, and at the Olympics.

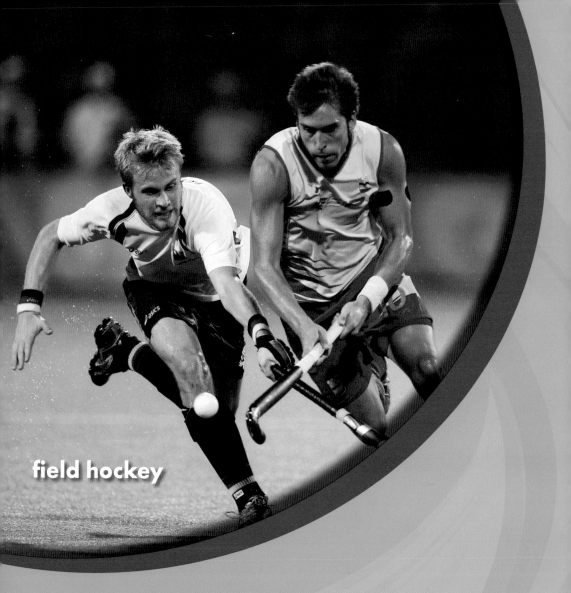

field hockey

People have been playing **field hockey** for hundreds of years. These games eventually moved onto ice, and players soon started using ice skates. In 1875, Canadian James George Creighton wrote the first modern hockey rule book.

fun fact

The early NHL included only Canadian teams. In 1924, the NHL expanded into the United States.

In 1893, teams began competing for a trophy called the Dominion Hockey Challenge Cup. It was later renamed the **Stanley Cup**. In 1917, the National Hockey League (NHL) was formed. Each year, the best team in the NHL wins the Stanley Cup.

The Basic Rules of Hockey

puck

goaltender

In a hockey game, two teams compete to score goals over three **periods**. Each period is 20 minutes long. A team scores by shooting a **puck** into the other team's goal. The team with the most goals at the end of the game wins.

In the NHL, a hockey team can have six players on the ice at a time. The **goaltender** guards the goal. Two **wingers** and a **center** score goals for the team. Two **defensemen** try to keep the other team from scoring.

A player sometimes breaks the rules and gets called for a **penalty**. A player who gets a penalty is sent to the penalty box for a set time. During that time, the other team is on a **power play**. They have a better chance to score because the other team has one less player. Most power plays last two minutes.

fun fact

In the NHL, if teams are tied after three periods, they go into overtime. Overtime lasts five minutes. If the game is still tied after overtime, it goes to a shoot-out. Shooters and goalies go one-on-one to decide the winner.

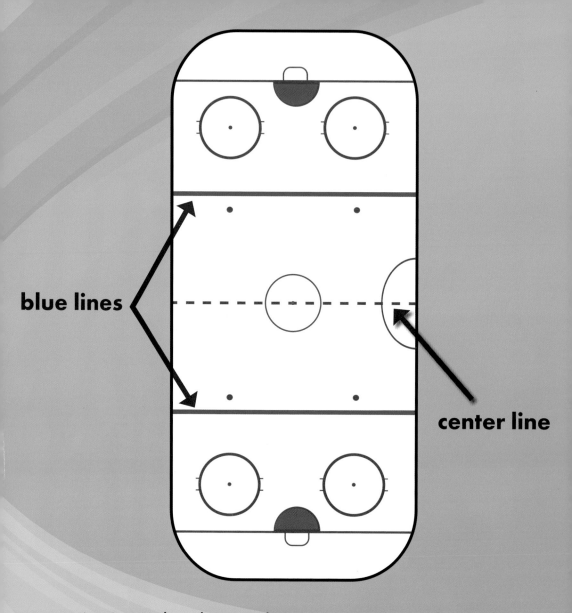

blue lines

center line

An NHL hockey rink measures 200 feet (61 meters) long and 85 feet (26 meters) wide. A dotted red line marks **center ice**. Each team has a zone to defend at either end of the rink. Blue lines mark these zones.

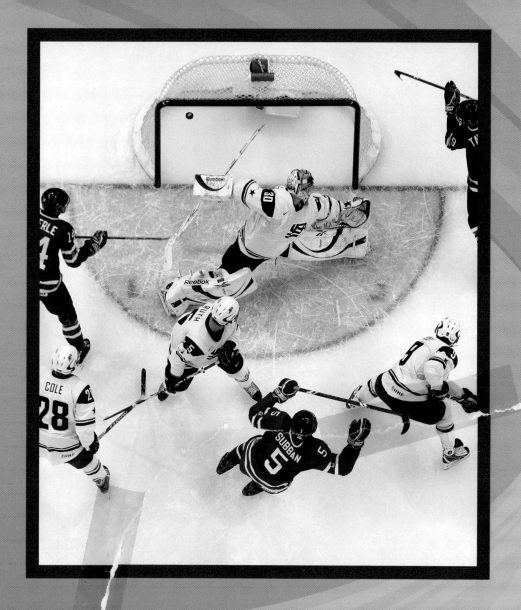

The goal is near the back of each team's zone. A red goal line is in front of the goal. The puck must pass the goal line to count as a goal.

Hockey Equipment

The puck is a black disk made of hard rubber. An NHL puck measures 3 inches (7.6 centimeters) across and is about 1 inch (2.5 centimeters) thick.

Players use hockey sticks to move the puck over the ice. Sticks can be made of wood, **carbon fiber**, and other materials.

All players wear ice skates. A single blade
on the bottom of each skate helps the
players glide over the ice.

Hockey can be a rough game. Players need protection. They wear helmets with face masks. They wear pads over most of their bodies. Goaltenders wear extra padding to protect them from hard shots.

Hockey Today

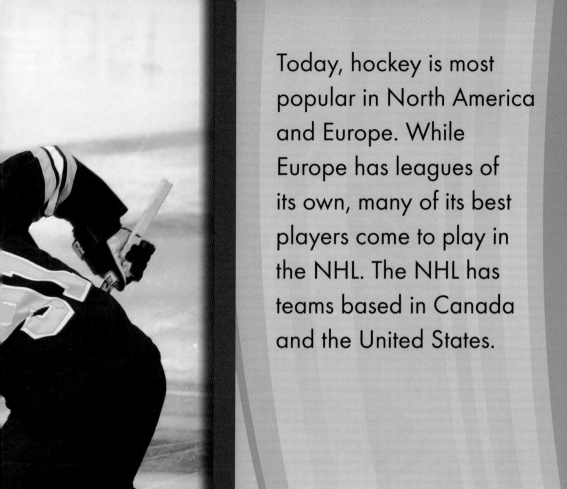

Today, hockey is most popular in North America and Europe. While Europe has leagues of its own, many of its best players come to play in the NHL. The NHL has teams based in Canada and the United States.

fun fact

Each hockey period begins with a face-off. A player from each team battles for control of a puck that a referee drops onto the ice.

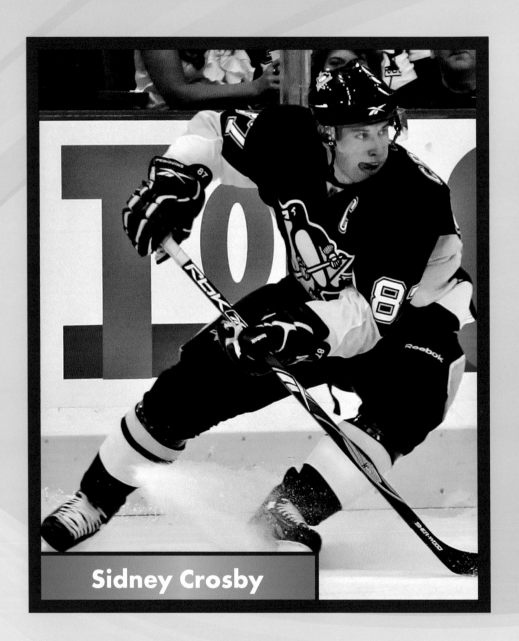

Sidney Crosby

NHL players like Sidney Crosby and Alexander Ovechkin excite fans with their smooth skating and pinpoint shooting.

Alexander Ovechkin

Men and women of all ages love to lace up their skates and compete in leagues at every level. Hockey has many fans—on and off the bench!

Glossary

carbon fiber—a tough, lightweight material used to make some hockey sticks

center—a player whose main job is to score goals and who often takes the face-off

center ice—the middle of the rink where the opening face-off for each period is held

defenseman—a player whose main job is to defend his or her team's own zone

field hockey—a sport similar to ice hockey in which players try to score goals on an open field

goaltender—the player who stands in front of the goal and tries to keep the other team from scoring

penalty—the punishment for breaking game rules; players who get a penalty are sent to the penalty box.

period—a length of time; a hockey game is made up of three periods of 20 minutes each.

power play—when one team has six players on the ice while the other team has five or fewer due to a penalty or penalties

puck—a small black disk made of hard rubber

Stanley Cup—the trophy awarded each year to the best team in the NHL

winger—a player whose main job is to score goals

To Learn More

AT THE LIBRARY
Doeden, Matt. *The Greatest Hockey Records*.
Mankato, Minn.: Capstone, 2008.

Fauchald, Nick. *Face Off! You Can Play Hockey*.
Minneapolis, Minn.: Picture Window Books, 2006.

Thomas, Keltie, and John Kicksee. *Inside Hockey!:
The Legends, Facts, and Feats that Made the Game*.
Ontario, Canada: Maple Tree Press, 2008.

ON THE WEB
Learning more about hockey
is as easy as 1, 2, 3.

1. Go to www.factsurfer.com.

2. Enter "hockey" into the search box.

3. Click the "Surf" button and you will see a list of
   related Web sites.

With factsurfer.com, finding more information is just a
click away.

Index

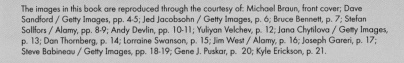